MW01131568

American Lives

Roger Williams

Elizabeth Raum

Heinemann Library
Chicago, Illinois

Customer Service 888-454-2279
Visit our website at www.heinemannlibrary.com

Designed by Heinemann Library
Photo research by Bill Broyles
Printed and bound in China by WKT Company
Limited

09 08 07 06 05
10 9 8 7 6 5 4 3 2 1

Library of Congress Cataloging-in-Publication Data
Raum, Elizabeth.
  Roger Williams / by Elizabeth Raum.
    v. cm. -- (American lives)
  Includes bibliographical references and index.
  Contents: Childhood -- Puritan law clerk --
Chaplain -- Escape from England -- Massachusetts --
Plymouth -- Salem -- Banished -- Providence --
Pequot war -- Rhode Island colony.
  ISBN 1-4034-5961-4 (HC), 1-4034-5969-X (Pbk)
  1. Williams, Roger, 1604?-1683--Juvenile literature.
2. Puritans--Rhode Island--Biography--Juvenile
literature. 3. Baptists--Rhode Island--Biography--
Juvenile literature. 4. Separatists--Rhode Island--
Biography--Juvenile literature. 5. Pioneers--Rhode
Island--Biography--Juvenile literature. 6. Rhode
Island--History--Colonial period, ca. 1600-1775--
Juvenile literature. [1. Williams, Roger, 1604?-1683.
2. Puritans. 3. Separatists. 4. Reformers. 5. Freedom
of religion. 6. Rhode Island--History--Colonial
period, ca. 1600-1775.] I. Title. II. Series: American
lives (Heinemann Library (Firm))

F82.W7R38 2004
974.5'02'092--dc22
                    2003027785

Acknowledgments
The author and publishers are grateful to the
following for permission to reproduce copyright
material:

Cover photograph by Bettmann/Corbis

Title page, p. 25 Courtesy of Roger Williams
University, Bristol, Rhode Island; p. 4 The
Bridgeman Art Library; p. 5 Courtesy of Roger
Williams University, Bristol, Rhode Island/Peter
Finger, photographer; p. 6 Hulton-Deutsch
Collection/Corbis; p. 7 Mary Evans Picture Library;
p. 8 Michael S. Yamashita/Corbis; p. 9 The Stapleton
Collection/The Bridgeman Art Library; pp. 10-14,
16-20, 22-24, 27-29 Bettmann/Corbis; p. 15 Dave G.
Houser/Corbis; p. 26 Courtesy Applewood Books,
reprint edition, 1997

The author would like to thank Diane Vendetti,
Education Director, and the staff of the Providence
Preservation Society for their advice and support.
She would also like to thank her editor, Angela
McHaney Brown, for her assistance with this
manuscript.

The publisher would like to thank Michelle Rimsa
for her comments in the preparation of this book.

Every effort has been made to contact copyright
holders of any material reproduced in this book.
Any omissions will be rectified in subsequent
printings if notice is given to the publisher.

For more information about the image of Roger
Williams that appears on the cover of this book, turn
to page 29.

Contents

Some words are shown in bold, **like this.** You can find out what they mean by looking in the glossary.

Childhood

When Roger Williams was a child in England, people were fighting about the right way to worship God. Roger studied the Bible and listened to what people said. When he was young, he joined a group called the **Puritans.**

Many Puritans, including the people we call the Pilgrims, were forced to leave England for North America. Roger left, too. He hoped that North America would be a place where people could worship God in whatever way they chose.

London was already a very busy city in the early 1600s.

This statue of Roger Williams is at Roger Williams University in Bristol, Rhode Island.

Roger was born in about 1603 in London, England. His father, James, was a **merchant tailor.** His shop was in the front of the family's house on Cow Lane. Cow Lane was home to many shops selling cloth, leather, and horse-drawn coaches. Roger's mother was named Alice. He had two brothers, Sydrach and Robert, and a sister, Katherine. Young Roger met all kinds of people, both rich and poor, in the busy streets of London.

Languages

*As a boy Roger learned English, **Latin,** and Dutch. Latin was used for business and law. Dutch was used by the cloth weavers who came to England from the Netherlands.*

Puritan Law Clerk

When Roger was eight years old, a Bible called the King James Bible was printed. It was written in English. Roger learned to read and write using the new Bible.

Like many boys his age, Roger learned **shorthand,** a system of speed writing. Sir Edward Coke was a famous lawyer who hired thirteen-year-old Roger to take shorthand notes during trials.

Puritans came before the throne to speak with King James I of England.

For five years Roger listened to Coke argue in court. Coke was a **Puritan** who made Roger study the Bible and read other important books. Roger learned about law and **religion** from Coke. Coke liked Roger and treated him like a son.

This illustration shows a trial that was held in London in 1641.

Chaplain

When Roger was eighteen, Coke sent him to the Charterhouse School. Roger spent two years there studying **Greek, Latin,** writing, **philosophy,** and **religion.** He went on to Cambridge University. Roger worked hard at his studies and graduated with honors in 1627. He stayed at Cambridge to study to become a **minister.**

Roger left school when he was 26. He became a **chaplain,** or minister, at the home of Sir William Masham. The Mashams lived in a large house in the country.

Cambridge University is located in Cambridge, England.

This English illustration from the 1600s is meant to show the ideal, happy marriage.

In the job of chaplain, Roger led the Sunday worship service, gave lectures, and held prayer meetings. He also read the Bible aloud to the family and taught the children.

In 1629 Roger became ill with a fever. Mary Barnard, a maid, visited him while he recovered. The two fell in love. On December 15, 1629, they were married.

Escape from England

During the 1620s, the English king put many **Puritans** in prison. Others fled to Holland, and from there some Puritans traveled to North America. While he was **chaplain** to the Mashams, Roger Williams met a Puritan **merchant** named John Winthrop. He also met John Cotton, an important Puritan **minister.**

These men were setting up the Massachusetts Bay Colony. They wanted the colony to be a safe place for Puritans to work and live. John Winthrop became the first governor of Massachusetts.

John Winthrop is shown here off the shore of Salem, Massachusetts.

The Life of Roger Williams

1603	1627	1629	1630	1632
Born in London, England	Graduated from Cambridge University	Married Mary Barnard	Sailed to Massachusetts	Worked as a missionary among Native Americans

It was common for Puritan ministers to preach to the people on the ships heading for North America.

As a Puritan minister, Roger was not safe in England. He and Mary hoped to practice their faith in Massachusetts. In early December 1630, Roger and Mary left England. It took the ship, called the *Lyon*, about two months to cross the Atlantic Ocean. It was a cold, difficult journey. The ship arrived on February 5, 1631. Governor Winthrop declared a day of thanksgiving on February 22 to **celebrate** the safe arrival of the 20 passengers and 200 **tons** of supplies.

1635	1636	1643	1654	c. 1683
Banished from Massachusetts Bay Colony	*Established Providence, Rhode Island*	*Wrote A Key into the Language of America*	*Became president of Rhode Island Colony*	*Died in Providence*

Massachusetts

Boston church leaders offered Roger Williams the job of **minister** and teacher. They did not know that before leaving England, Williams had become a **Separatist.** Like other Separatists, Williams wanted to separate from the **Church of England.** He believed that the church and the **state,** or government, should be separate from one another.

Pilgrims at Plymouth met regularly to hold church services.

Puritan Punishment

*In Boston if someone broke a church law, the **magistrates** could punish that person. For example, if people swore or worked on Sunday, they might be put in the **stocks**, a wooden frame used for punishment.*

People in Boston were punished in stocks in the town square. Other people were expected to learn from their example.

The more he talked about his Separatist beliefs, the more upset Boston's church leaders became. Williams turned down the job of minister to the Boston church. He said he could not work among people who did not believe as he did. Church leaders in Salem invited Williams to become a minister there and welcomed him to their town and church.

Plymouth

Roger and Mary Williams moved to Salem. Williams worked there for less than a year before moving to Plymouth to be an assistant **minister.** The people of Plymouth agreed with Williams' ideas.

While in Plymouth, Williams was friendly to the Narrangansett, Wampanoag, and Neponset people who lived in the area. He learned their languages and their **customs.** Unlike other **colonists,** he cared about the Native Americans and listened to what they said. He preached to both colonists and Native Americans.

This is an illustration of everyday life in Plymouth.

A 1627 Pilgrim Village has been recreated and can be toured at the Plymouth Plantation Museum.

Williams questioned the right of the **Puritan** colonists to take Native American land. He said that the colonists must pay for the land if the Native Americans were willing to sell it. If not, the colonists must move. This idea worried the leaders in Plymouth and Boston. They had a **charter** from the king that gave them the right to carry on trade in New England. However, it did not allow them to take Native American land.

Salem

In 1633 Roger and Mary Williams returned to Salem. Their first child, Mary, was born in August. Williams worked as a church teacher. He also owned a house in Salem and farmed his land. He traded with Dutch **merchants** and Native Americans. He continued to preach and teach in Salem until August of 1635. He also wrote a paper explaining why he did not agree with the rules of the Massachusetts Bay Colony.

Pilgrims are shown here meeting peacefully with a group of Native Americans.

These were the typical clothing styles of a Puritan family.

Williams said that people should be able to choose whatever **religion** they wished or no religion at all. He did not agree that everyone should be forced to attend church or that the government should punish those who did not. He believed that people should have the freedom to worship as they chose. He was the first to stand up for **religious freedom** in the North American colonies.

Sent Away

Willliams wrote letters to the churches in Massachusetts complaining about **ministers** who disagreed with him. The letters made church leaders angry. They brought Williams to trial for preaching dangerous ideas. John Cotton spoke against him during the trial. On October 9, 1635, the court found Williams guilty of preaching dangerous ideas. They **banished** him, ordering him to leave the Massachusetts Bay Colony forever.

John Cotton (1584–1652) had been Roger Williams's friend before the trial.

Roger Williams had to travel through the surrounding wilderness after being cast out of the Massachusetts Bay Colony.

After the trial, Williams became ill. The court let him stay in Massachusetts until he was well, as long as he did not preach. But as soon as he felt better, he began to preach again. The leaders sent someone to put Williams on a ship to England.

Governor Winthrop, who liked Williams, told him of the plan. Williams left Salem alone during the night. Mary, who was expecting another child, remained in Massachusetts until spring.

Providence

Narrangansett Indians helped Williams find a place to start his new colony.

Roger Williams walked through deep snow into the forest. For fourteen weeks, Native Americans gave him food and shelter. When Williams reached Narrangansett Bay in 1636, he **founded** a new settlement named Providence. Two Narrangansett chiefs named Canonicus and Miantonomo gave the land to Williams. When other settlers arrived, the chiefs gave them seeds and food. That spring, Mary Williams arrived with a new baby. She was named Freeborn because she had been born free from the rules of the Boston **Puritans.**

Roger Williams's Firsts

- *First to call for the separation of church and state in North America*
- *First to start a colony, Rhode Island, where all religious groups were welcome*
- *First to found the city of Providence, Rhode Island*
- *First to found a Baptist church in North America*

Williams invited anyone who wanted to join him to live free in Rhode Island. He set up a government that was separate from the church. People could worship however they wanted. Williams became a **Baptist** and in 1638 founded the first Baptist church in North America in Providence. Later, he called himself a Seeker because he was **seeking** the truth about God.

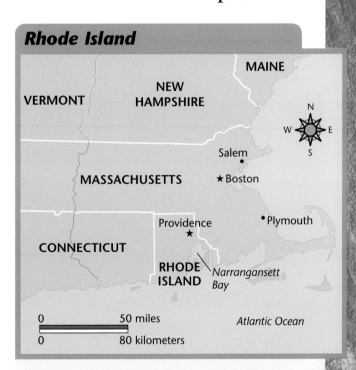

Rhode Island

VERMONT

NEW HAMPSHIRE

MAINE

Salem

MASSACHUSETTS

★Boston

Providence ★

• Plymouth

CONNECTICUT

RHODE ISLAND

Narrangansett Bay

Atlantic Ocean

0   50 miles
0   80 kilometers

It would have been difficult to form Rhode Island without the help of Native Americans.

Pequot War

Soon after Roger Williams arrived in Providence, a war broke out between the English **colonists** and the Pequot Indians. The Pequots, who lived east of the Connecticut River, wanted the Narrangansetts' land. The English colonists and the Narragansetts fought together. The Pequots began attacking English traders, and the colonists prepared to fight back.

Townspeople often had to secure their homes against attacks by Native Americans.

Williams was known for his good relationships with Native Americans, as shown in this illustration.

Everyone, both the English colonists of Massachusetts Bay Colony and the Native Americans, considered Williams the most important man in New England. If anyone could stop the war, it was Williams. He left Providence on a stormy night, alone in a canoe, and headed to the Pequot village. For three days and nights he lived with them.

After much talk, he worked out a peace treaty between the English and the Narrangansetts. Williams was a great friend to the Native Americans. He always told the colonists to treat Native Americans with **respect** and kindness.

Rhode Island Colony

By 1640 there were 40 families living in Providence. Roger Williams farmed his land and traded with the Native Americans. The Native Americans considered him a good man. They visited often. Sometimes as many as 50 stayed in the Williams' home in Providence. Because Williams was not allowed to go to Boston to buy goods and supplies, he traveled to New York to trade with the Dutch settlers who lived there.

Williams is shown here being welcomed by Native Americans on one of his trading visits.

Roger Williams knew that a royal charter would help protect his colony.

In May 1643, Williams sailed for England, leaving his wife, who was expecting another baby, and five children behind. He wanted to get a **charter** for Rhode Island from the king of England. **Colonists** from Massachusetts were trying to take land in Rhode Island. It took almost a year to get the charter. By the time Williams returned home, his newest son had been born. Roger and Mary Williams now had six children.

Author

While sailing to England, Roger Williams had written a book called *A Key into the Language of America.* It explained Native American languages and **customs.** Throughout his life, he tried to defend Native Americans against **colonists** who wanted to take their land.

ROGER WILLIAMS

A Key into the LANGUAGE *of* AMERICA

Edited with a Critical Introduction, Notes, and Commentary by John J. Teunissen and Evelyn J. Hinz

After moving to Rhode Island, Williams stopped trying to make Native Americans become **Christians.** He respected their customs and traditions without trying to change them.

Williams's book on Native American languages was first published in 1643.

Anne Hutchinson was placed on trial for her religious beliefs.

The next year, in 1644, Williams wrote a book called *The Bloody Tenet of Persecution*. This book explained his religious ideas in founding Rhode Island. Williams' Rhode Island was home to many religious groups. Among the first was Anne Hutchinson and her followers. They arrived in 1638 after being **banished** from Boston. Hutchinson founded Portsmouth, Rhode Island. **Quakers** came, too. Even though Williams argued with them about their ideas, he defended their right to worship as they wanted.

Religious Freedom

This was Roger William's house while he was the governor of Rhode Island.

In 1654 Roger Williams was elected president of the colony of Rhode Island. Whenever the freedom of Rhode Island was in danger, Williams took action. He made sure that **religious freedom** was protected.

Jews in Rhode Island

In 1656, while Williams was governor of Rhode Island, the first Jewish synagogue in North American was built in Newport, Rhode Island.

As he grew older, the job of keeping Rhode Island free and safe made Williams tired and sick. But he never gave up his dream.

The exact date of Williams's death is not known. It is believed that he died in 1683 at the age of 80. His ideas about religious freedom and the separation of church and **state** continue to this day.

Williams's ideas about religious freedom were later written into the U.S. Bill of Rights.

Glossary

banished   sent out of a town or country

Baptists   Christian group that believes that only people old enough to understand its meaning should be baptized

celebrate   to be festive

chaplain   religious leader

charter   agreement or permission

Christian   person who follows the teachings of Jesus Christ

Church of England   national church in England

colonist   original settler of a new place

customs   usual way of behaving

founded   formally started

Greek   language of people who lived in ancient Greece

Jews   people who follow Judaism, the religion of the ancient Hebrews

Jewish   relating to the Jews

Latin   language of people who lived in ancient Rome

magistrate   city judge

merchant   businessman

minister   religious leader

philosophy   study of knowledge

Protestant   Christian who is not Catholic

Puritans   group that wanted to change the Church of England

Quakers   Christian group that began in England; also called the Society of Friends

religion   belief in a god or gods

religious freedom   right to worship as one chooses

respect   to honor

seeking   looking for

Separatists   group that wanted to separate from the
   Church of England

shorthand   system of speed writing

state   government

stock   wooden frame used to punish people

synagogue   Jewish house of worship

tailor   person who makes clothes

ton   2,000 pounds

More Books to Read

Avi. *Finding Providence: The Story of Roger Williams.*
   New York: HarperCollins, 1997.

An older reader can help you with this book:

Allison, Amy. *Roger Williams.* Mankato, Minn.:
   Chelsea House, 2000.

Places to Visit

Roger Williams National Memorial
   282 North Main Street
   Providence, Rhode Island 02903
   Visitor Information: (401) 521-7266

Plimoth Plantation
   137 Warren Street
   Plymouth, Massachusetts 02360
   Visitor Information: (508) 746-1622

Index